PIANO/VOCAL SELECTIONS

Michael Bennett, Bob Avian, Geffen Rec
and the Shubert Organization
present

DREAMGIRLS

Book and Lyrics by
Tom Eyen

Music by
Henry Krieger

starring

Obba Babatunde • Cleavant Derricks • Loretta Devine
Ben Harney • Jennifer Holliday • Sheryl Lee Ralph

with

Deborah Burrell • Vondie Curtis-Hall • Tony Franklin • David Thome

Scenic Design	Costume Design	Lighting Design	Sound Design
Robin Wagner	Theoni V. Aldredge	Tharon Musser	Otts Munderloh

Musical Supervision and Orchestrations by
Harold Wheeler

Musical Director
Yolanda Segovia

Vocal Arrangements
Cleavant Derricks

Hair Styles
Ted Azar

Productions Stage Manager
Jeff Hamlin

General Manager
Marvin A. Krauss

Co-Choreographer
Michael Peters

Directed and Choreographed by
Michael Bennett

ISBN-13: 978-1-4234-1616-6
ISBN-10: 1-4234-1616-3

HAL•LEONARD®
CORPORATION
7777 W. BLUEMOUND RD. P.O. BOX 13819 MILWAUKEE, WI 53213

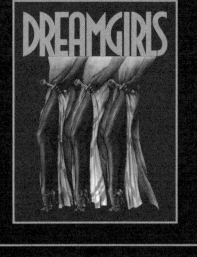

CONTENTS

MOVE
(You're Stepping on My Heart)

Music by HENRY KRIEGER
Lyric by TOM EYEN

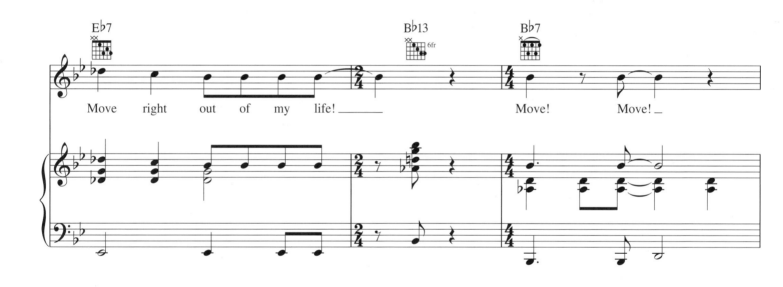

FAKE YOUR WAY TO THE TOP

Music by HENRY KRIEGER
Lyric by TOM EYEN

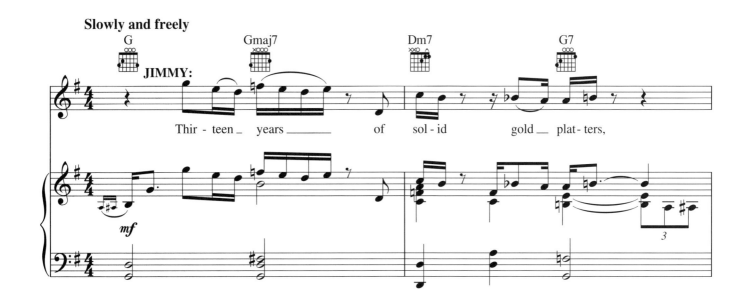

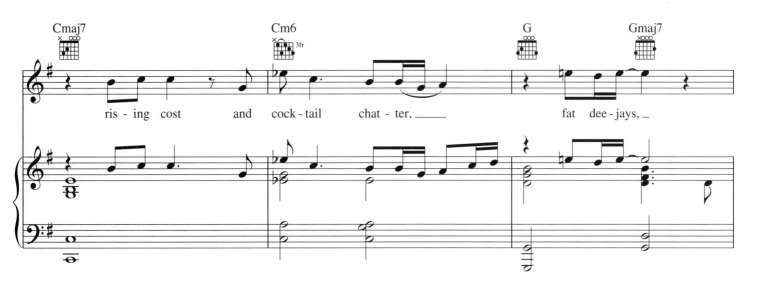

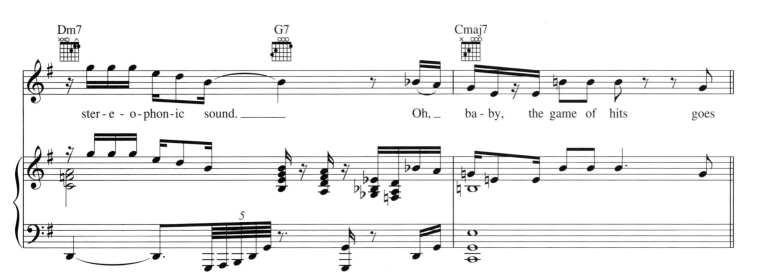

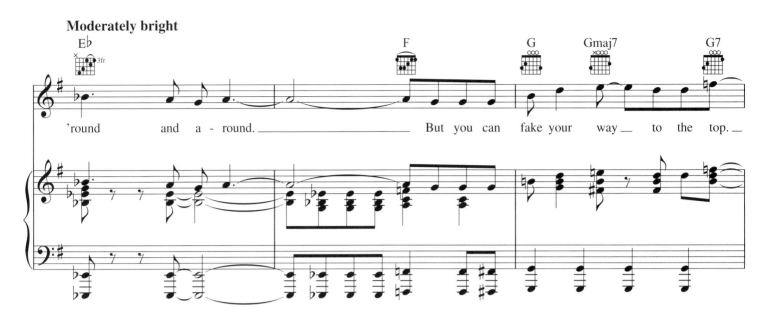

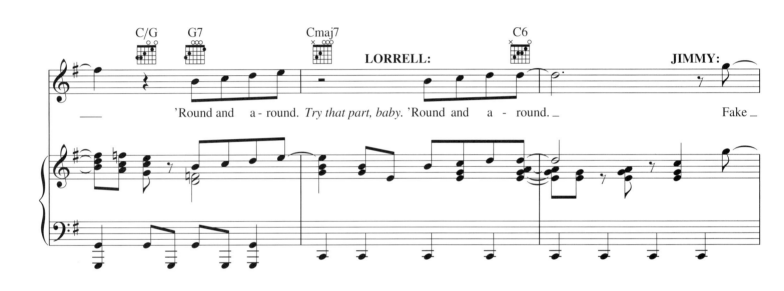

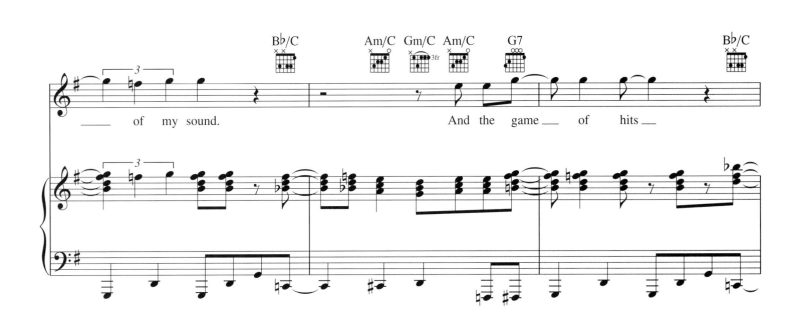

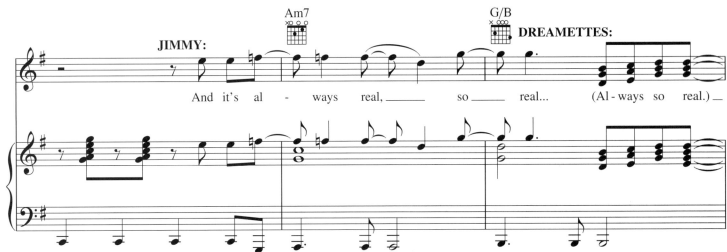

CADILLAC CAR

Music by HENRY KRIEGER
Lyric by TOM EYEN

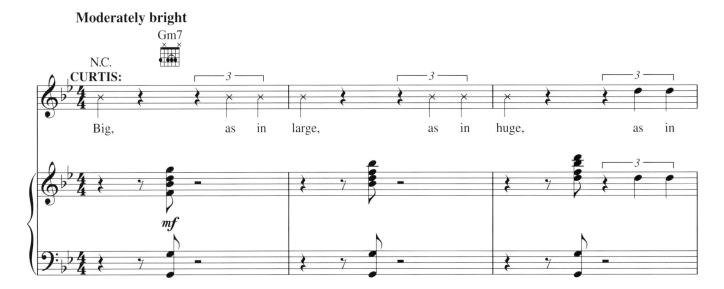

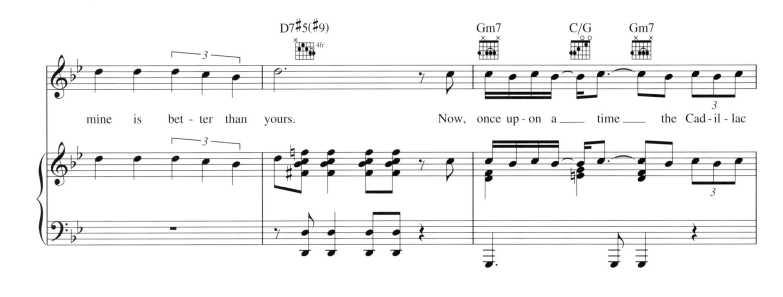

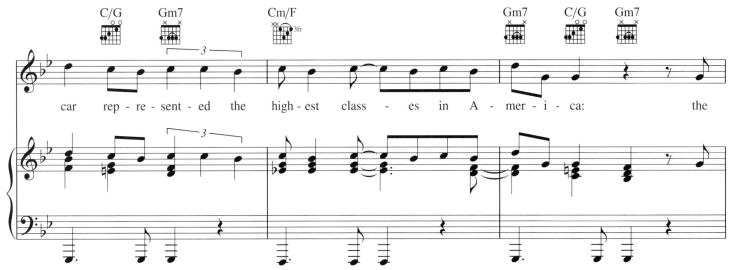

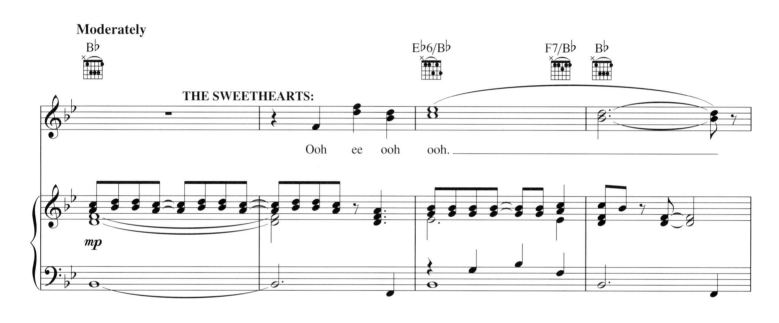

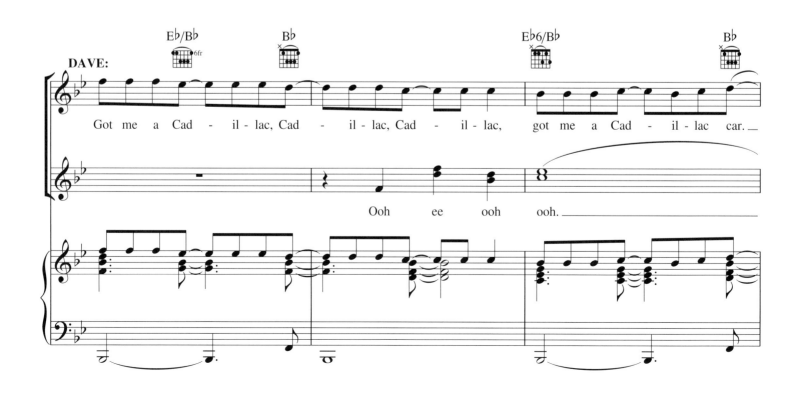

STEPPIN' TO THE BAD SIDE

Music by HENRY KRIEGER
Lyric by TOM EYEN

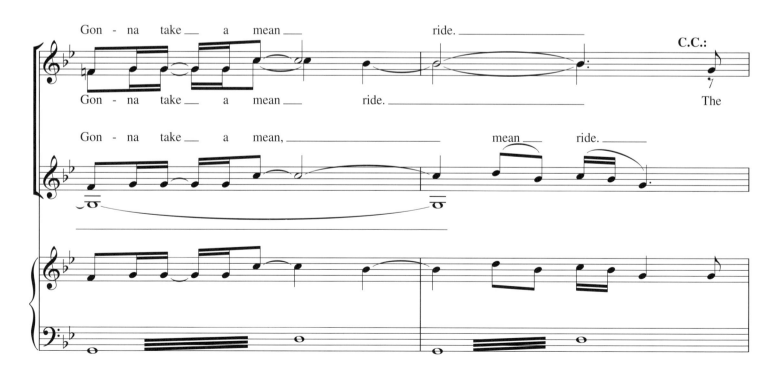

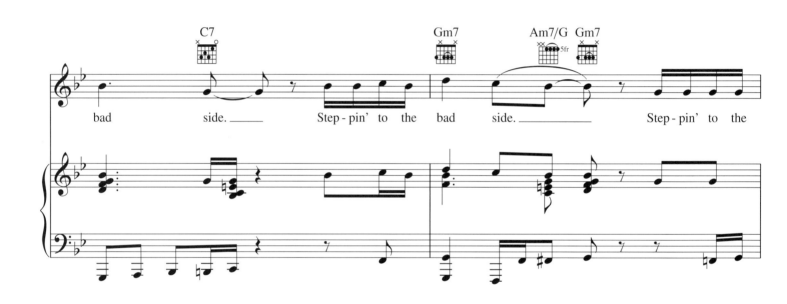

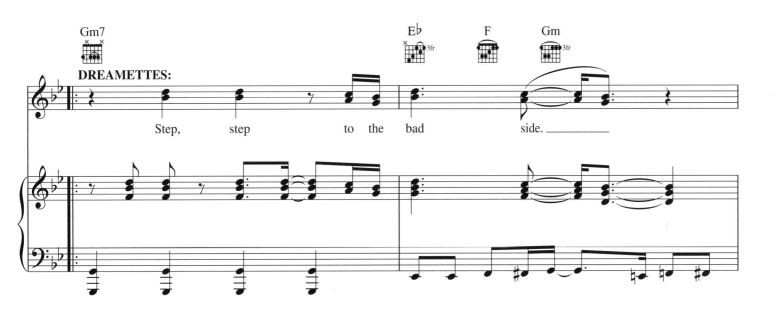

I WANT YOU, BABY

Music by HENRY KRIEGER
Lyric by TOM EYEN

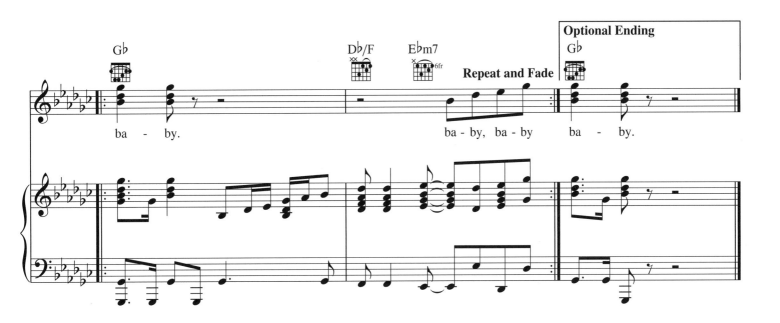

FAMILY

Music by HENRY KRIEGER
Lyric by TOM EYEN

DREAMGIRLS

Music by HENRY KRIEGER
Lyric by TOM EYEN

HEAVY

Music by HENRY KRIEGER
Lyric by TOM EYEN

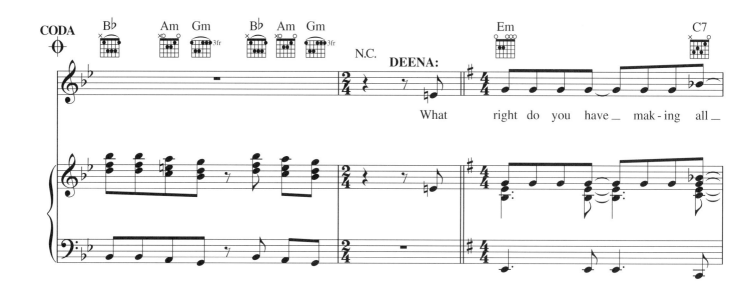

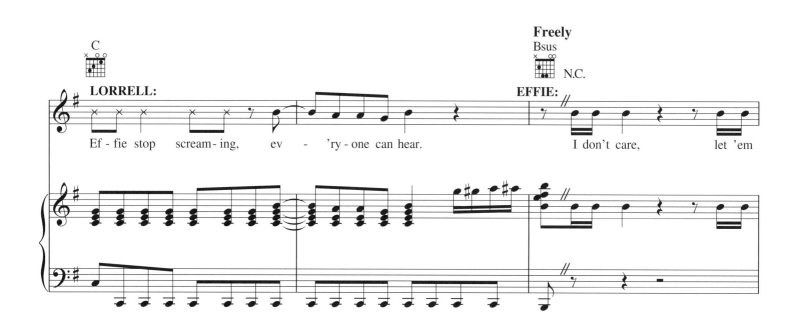

Tempo II

warn - ing you, now, ___ stop bring - in' us down. ___ Stop bring - in' us ___

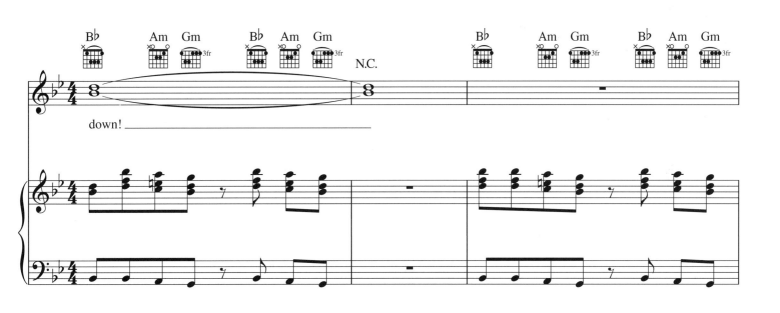

down! ___

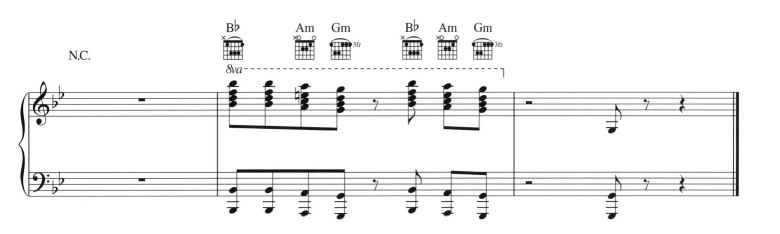

AND I AM TELLING YOU I'M NOT GOING

Music by HENRY KRIEGER
Lyric by TOM EYEN

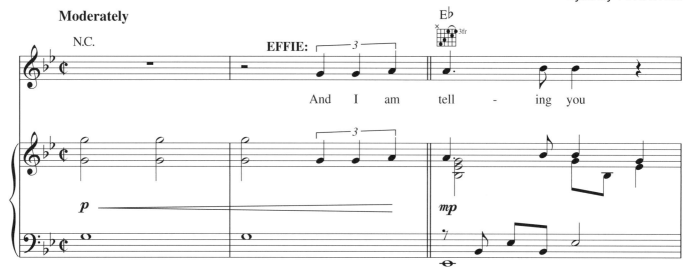

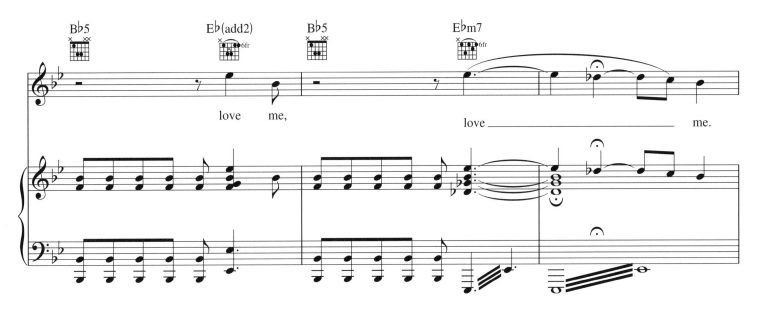

love me, love _____ me.

Freely

N.C.

You're gon - na love _____

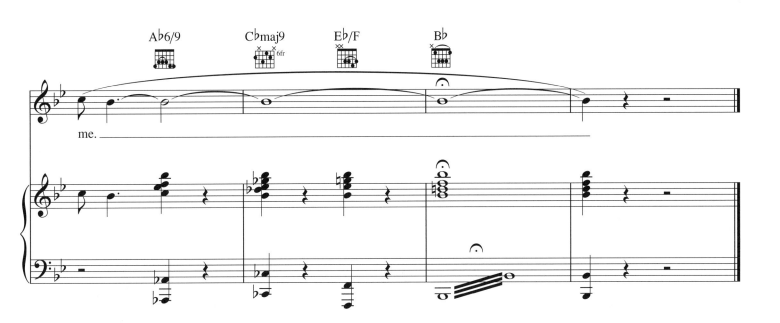

me. _____

I AM CHANGING

Music by HENRY KRIEGER
Lyric by TOM EYEN

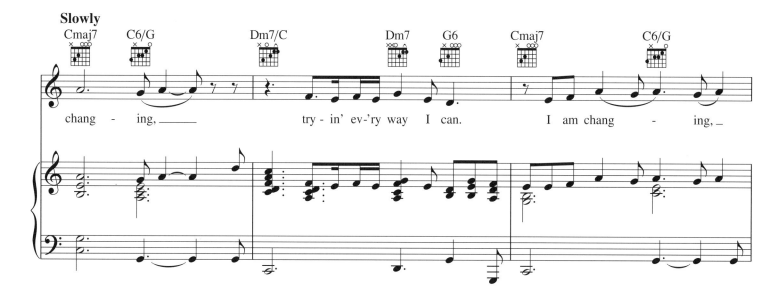

WHEN I FIRST SAW YOU

Music by HENRY KRIEGER
Lyric by TOM EYEN

Moderately slow and free

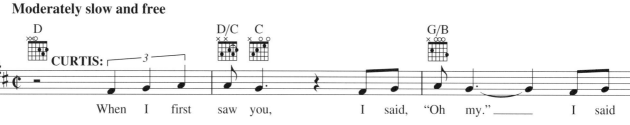

CURTIS: When I first saw you, I said, "Oh my." ___ I said

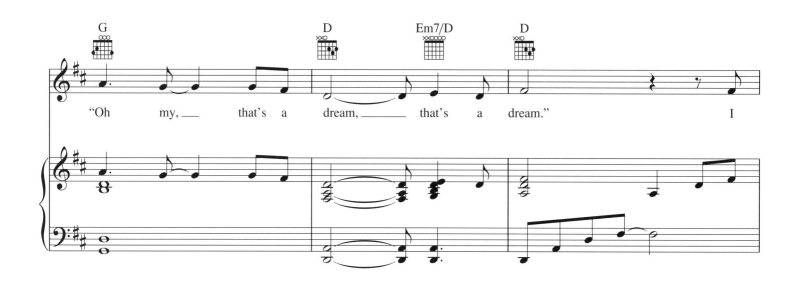

"Oh my, ___ that's a dream, ___ that's a dream." I

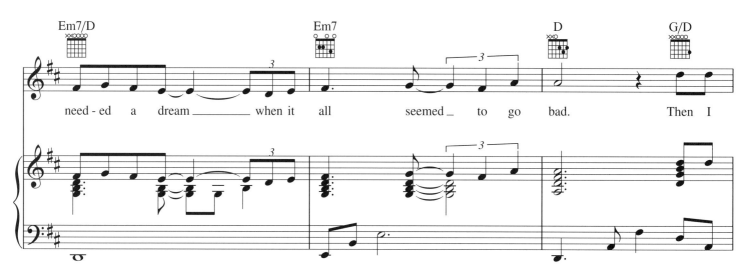

need-ed a dream ___ when it all seemed ___ to go bad. Then I

AIN'T NO PARTY

Music by HENRY KRIEGER
Lyric by TOM EYEN

LORRELL: Yes, I knew you were mar - ried when I met you. Told __ my - self that's the way it's got to be. But af - ter

ONE NIGHT ONLY

Music by HENRY KRIEGER
Lyric by TOM EYEN

HARD TO SAY GOODBYE, MY LOVE

Music by HENRY KRIEGER
Lyric by TOM EYEN